Digital Natives

Blockchain, NFT, Cryptocurrency

Illustrated by **Sienny Septibella**

X.30 and Y.5- are best friends and live in a digital world called Metaverse where there are no borders, countries, governments or nationalities.

We live in a decentralised world!

There are **communities** called *cryptocurrencies* and *exchanges*, that live on different *layers* of blockchain technology.

The **blockchain** is an **encrypted network** of **codes** that stores **information**, which are **chained together** to form a **long chain of blocks**.

No single organisation or *individual* owns the blockchain, and *multiple blockchains* exist!

The **public key** can be shared with others, allowing *digital assets* to be *sent* and *received*.

The *private key* is a *password*, used to *sign transactions* and prove *ownership* of the *digital assets* inside our *wallet*.

An *NFT* is a *one-of-a-kind digital asset created* and *traded* through *blockchain technology.*

X.30 and Y.5- spend their days *minting NFTs* on blockchain platforms like *Ethereum* and *Polygon.*

To make transactions in the Metaverse, X.30 and Y.5- use a virtual form of payment called cryptocurrency, also known as digital coins.

The first cryptocurrency created is called Bitcoin (BTC). Another popular cryptocurrency is called Ether (ETH).

 Did you know that there are 1 million bits in 1 bitcoin?

Physical money used on Earth is called *fiat* or *fiat currency*.

At an *exchange,* you can *buy* different cryptocurrencies with fiat, *change* Bitcoin to Ether and *convert* cryptocurrencies back into fiat.

Some blockchains consume *much less energy* than mining through *randomly-selected beings* (also known as *validators*), who do not need any equipment to solve puzzles!

When an NFT design is ready, creators link their wallet to a blockchain platform, like Ethereum or Polygon.

This process is called minting!

They also choose an *NFT marketplace* that *supports* their selected blockchain platform. After this, they *upload* the *digital file* to the NFT marketplace.

The digital file now becomes a *digital asset (NFT)*.

Blockchain technology verifies and stores a record of the creator of the NFT and its subsequent transactions, should it be bought or traded.

Some buy NFTs to *support creators* or for the *love of art,* and others as an *investment.*

Y.5- holds one of the *largest collections* of Bored Ape Yacht Club! Each NFT depicts an ape or cat with *different traits* and *visual attributes.*

Glossary

Blockchain

Decentralised, distributed, public ledger that stores data and records the provenance of every digital asset or transaction made on its network

 88

Burn

Removing NFTs from circulation by sending them to a wallet address that no one owns or has access to

 78

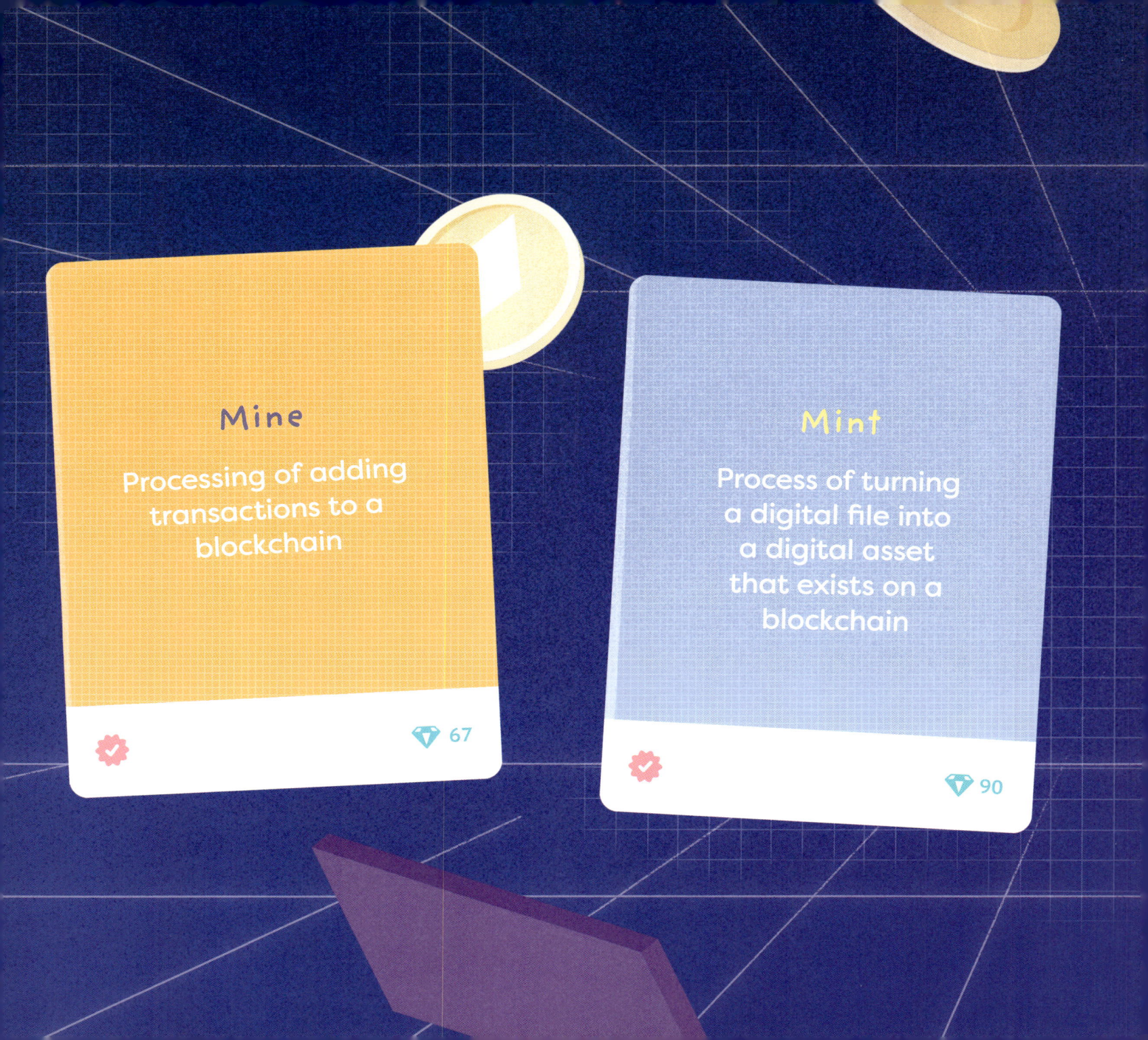

cinnamon
art stories

First published in 2023 by Cinnamon Art Publishing
www.cinnamonartstories.com

Text © Cinnamon Art Publishing
Illustrations © Cinnamon Art Publishing

Text by Cinnamon Art Publishing
Illustrations by Sienny Septibella, Natasya Meredith (assistant)

Creative direction by Laura Peh
Art direction by Sienny Septibella

ISBN 978-981-18-3404-2

A catalogue record for this book is available from
the National Library Board Singapore.

All rights reserved. No part of this book may be reproduced, stored in a retrieval system, transmitted or utilised, in any form or by any means, electronic, mechanical, photocopying, recording or otherwise, now known or hereafter invented, including photocopying and recording, without the written permission of Cinnamon Art Publishing.

Printed in Turkey.